G000242237

Just

for

the

Craic

JUST FOR THE CRAIC

Summersdale Publishers Ltd
46 West Street
Chichester
West Sussex
PO19 1RP
UK

www.summersdale.com

Printed and bound in China

ISBN: 978-1-84953-351-5

Substantial discounts on bulk quantities of Summersdale books are available to corporations, professional associations and other organisations. For details contact Nicky Douglas by telephone: (+44-1243-756902), fax: (+44-1243-786300) or email: nicky@summersdale.com.

Just
for
the
Craic

THE VERY BEST IRISH JOKES

Cormac O'Brien

summersdale

Danny decided to take karate lessons so that he could kill a man with his bare feet.

On his way home one night, he was mugged, but by the time he got his shoes and socks off...

MURPHY:
me wife is driving me to drink!

SEAMUS:
you're lucky! mine makes me walk!

Brought up in the courts for drunk and disorderly behaviour, Mickey sits in the docks.

When asked, 'What do you have to say for yourself?' he replies, 'Your Honour, it must be said, I was sober enough to know that I was drunk.'

There are only

two types

of people in the world.

The Irish,

and those who

wish they were.

Paddy was walking into O'Sullivan's bar when he was shouted at by a nun. Sister Josephine said to him, 'Surely a fine young man like yourself wouldn't go into a den of iniquity like this, spending your money on the devil's brew rather than feeding and clothing your wife and children?'

'Now, Sister,' said Paddy, 'how can you condemn alcohol if you've never even tasted it yourself?'

'All right,' said Sister Josephine. 'Just to prove my point to you, I will taste the stuff this once. Of course, I can't go into the pub, so would you bring me out some gin? And put it in a cup, not a glass, to hide my intent.'

Now with a mission on his hands, Paddy walked into the bar and said to the barman, 'I'll have a large gin please, but in a cup rather than a glass.'

'Jesus,' said the barman, 'is that bloody nun outside again?'

O'Leary stood at the altar, swaying from side to side. What a way to be on your wedding day!

'This man is drunk!' said Father Casey to the bride.

'I know, Father,' she said. 'But sure he wouldn't have come if he was sober!'

Two brothers, Brendan and Jimmy, were sat watching TV together when the Tour de France came on.

'Why do they do that?' asked Brendan.

'Do what?' replied Jimmy.

'Cycle for all those miles, up and down, day after day, month after month in all weathers. Why do they torture themselves like that?'

'Because,' said Jimmy, 'the winner gets half a million euros!'

'Yes,' replied Brendan. 'But why do all the others do it?'

A man walked into a bar in Cork and asked the barman if he had heard the latest Kerryman joke.

'I'm warning you,' said the barman, 'I'm a Kerryman myself.'

'That's alright,' said the customer, 'I'll tell it slowly.'

A true Irishman

might not know

if there is a God,

but he's damn sure about

the infallibility

of the Pope.

THIS ESTABLISHMENT CLOSES AT 11 O'CLOCK SHARP. WE ARE OPEN FROM 10 A.M. UNTIL 11 P.M. AND IF YOU HAVEN'T HAD ENOUGH TO DRINK AT THAT HOUR THE MANAGEMENT FEELS THAT YOU HAVEN'T REALLY BEEN TRYING.

Sign on the door of an Irish pub

FINNEGAN:
my wife has a terrible habit of staying up till two o'clock in the morning. i can't break her out of it.

KEENAN:
what on earth is she doin' at that time?

FINNEGAN:
waitin' for me to come home.

Father McPhee walked into the church and spotted a man sitting cross-legged on the altar.

'My son,' said the priest, 'what are you doing? Who are you?'

'I'm God,' replied the strange man.

'I'm sorry?'

'I'm God,' he said again. 'This is my house!'

Father McPhee ran into the presbytery and, panicking, called the archbishop.

'Your Reverence,' he began, 'I'm sorry to trouble you, but there's a man sat on the altar here who claims he's God. What should I do?'

'Take no chances,' replied the archbishop. 'Go back into the church and look busy!'

'What are you getting your wife for Christmas?' Kelly asked O'Keefe.

'She decided for me,' said O'Keefe. 'She said she wanted something with diamonds in, so I've bought her a pack of cards!'

All women become like their mothers. That is their tragedy. No man does. That is his.

Oscar Wilde

An Englishman was driving past a small village just outside Dublin, and was surprised to see a sign that read:

WHEN YOU CAN'T READ THIS SIGN, THE ROAD IS FLOODED.

A man walked into a bar in Sydney and ordered a pint of Guinness.

'Excuse me,' said the only other customer. 'Is that an Irish accent I hear?'

'Yes, sor. Dublin to be exact.'

'Bedad,' said the first. 'I'm a Dubliner meself. Ballymun to be precise.'

'Jesus, I'm from Ballymun meself – Sother Street in fact,' said the second.

'Sother Street is where I was born and raised meself, and St Josephine's was me parish church, Father Delaney the parish priest.'

'I went to Mass every Sunday at St Josephine's. What a small world! Did you go to St Josephine's School?'

'I did. I was in Miss O'Malley's class.'

'Saints in heaven. Me too!'

Just then the phone rang and the barman answered, 'Not too busy at the moment. In fact there's just the Doolan twins here.'

BRIAN:
paddy, why is it that whenever you ask an irishman a question, he answers with another question?

PADDY:
who told you that?

You have to pity

the sober in the morning.

The way they're

feeling then is the best that

they'll feel all day!

‘What would you be if you weren’t Irish?’
asked the barman.

Pat replied, ‘Ashamed!’

At her brother's funeral, Niamh turned to her friend and said, 'Wasn't it tragic about my brother, Paul? Women and whiskey killed him.'

'Really?' said her sympathetic friend.

'Aye, he couldn't get either so he hung himself!'

An English tourist, out on a walk through the Kerry countryside, asked a farmer for help.

'How long will it take me to walk into the village from here?' asked the Englishman.

'No idea,' replied the farmer.

The tourist stormed off, muttering under his breath.

'Come back, sor,' called the Kerryman.

'What now?' snapped the tourist.

'It'll take ye about fifteen minutes.'

'Why didn't you tell me that in the first place?' asked the Englishman.

'Sure I didn't know how fast ye walked!' said the farmer with a smile.

Liam O'Donoghue had drunk more than enough Guinness and had stumbled out of Finn's bar and into the Sunday afternoon air.

As his drunken eyes squinted, an ambulance went by at great speed. Blue lights flashing and siren roaring, it sped up the street, with Liam running after it.

A hundred yards, two hundred, three hundred, almost a quarter of a mile he ran after it until finally, lungs and legs giving out, he fell into the gutter.

Then, with his last bit of breath he shouted, 'You can keep your ruddy ice cream!'

> ## THE SHOVELS HAVEN'T ARRIVED YET, AND UNTIL THEY DO, YOU'LL HAVE TO LEAN ON EACH OTHER!

Notice at a Dublin building site

'I'm not sure about this duck hunting,' said O'Toole. 'We've been here five hours and we still haven't caught one.'

'Maybe we're not throwing the dog high enough,' suggested Ronan.

DOCTOR:

you've nothing to
worry about. you
haven't got pneumonia.
it is only influenza.

CIAN:

doctor, please be honest
with me. did you not once
treat a man for influenza
who died of pneumonia.

DOCTOR:

my dear man. anybody i
ever treated for influenza
died from influenza. i do
not make mistakes.

Two drunks sat in a Dublin pub. Hung on the wall was a huge mirror, 14 feet long. Looking around the room, Barry suddenly spotted their reflection.

'Sean, Sean,' he said. 'There's two fellas over there who look just like us!'

'Jesus!' said Sean. 'They're wearing the same sorta clothes and everything. I'm going to have to buy those boys a drink!'

But, as Sean started to rise from his seat, Barry said, 'Sit down Sean, one of them's coming over here!'

Always an opportunist,
Cormac walked
all the way to the
heart of Australia
because he'd heard it was
virgin territory...

An Irish police officer in Liverpool found a dead horse in Cazneau Street. Not being too sure how to spell Cazneau Street he dragged the beast into Hill Street.

Two French counterfeiters had made thousands of genuine-looking notes – €50, €20, €10 – but they always wanted more. Scrambling through the discarded notes that had not passed scrutiny, they came upon a note that was completely perfect – except that it was for €18.

'Never mind,' said the boss. 'We'll unload it when we're over in Ireland.'

So they took the note with them and, whilst in Cork, they entered a corner shop to get rid of the note.

'Excuse me,' said the boss to shopkeeper O'Brien. 'Have you got change for an €18 note?'

'Indeed I have, sor,' said O'Brien. 'Would you like three sixes or two nines?'

Seamus walks into a fish and chip shop and says, 'I'll have cod and chips twice.'

'No problem,' said the shop assistant. 'The fish won't be long.'

'Then they'd better be fat!' replied Seamus.

Niall was getting irate and shouted upstairs to his wife, 'Hurry up or we'll be late.'

'Oh, be quiet, man.' replied his wife. 'Haven't I been telling you for the past hour that I'll be ready in a minute?'

The Kerry farmer

thought that the

Royal Mint was

what the Queen put on her

roast lamb.

Murphy went to the local cake shop and asked, 'Are the cream cakes fresh?'

'Oh yes,' said the baker. 'They're as fresh as the girl of your dreams!'

'In that case,' replied Murphy, 'I'd best have a meat pie.'

'I'm thinking of whitewashing the shed,' said Finn to the barman Pat O'Shea.

'What colour were you thinking of whitewashing it?' asked O'Shea.

'Well, I was thinking of whitewashing it green,' mused Finn. 'But I'm not sure if I can spare the time.'

'Why don't you let my lad do it for you,' suggested Pat. 'He'll whitewash it any colour you like. He won't charge you a penny and it'll be a few quid for the boy as well!'

The phone rang in a Dublin hospital casualty department.

'Hello,' said a frantic voice. 'It's Cormac Delany here. Can you come quickly, my wife is about to give birth.'

'I see,' said the receptionist at the end of the line. 'And is this her first child?'

'No!' exclaimed Delany. 'This is her husband speaking.'

FARMER'S SON:
we got a lecture on yeats
in school today, daddy.

FARMER:
and I suppose, ignorant
thing that you are,
you didn't even know
what a yeat was.

What do you call

an Irishman who knows how

to control his wife?

A bachelor.

'Why won't you marry me?' demanded Mickey. 'There isn't anyone else?'

'Oh, Mickey,' sighed Biddy. 'There must be.'

Paul O'Keefe was ill and his young son saw his mother sterilising the crockery that came from his room. He asked his mother what she was doing and she said, 'Daddy has germs and these get on the plates, so I boil the crockery so that the germs will be killed.'

Having thought for a while the boy asked, 'But Mammy, wouldn't it be handier to boil Daddy?'

An American tourist stood by watching an Irish farmer dig and turn over the soil. Eventually he called, 'Hey, pal, what's that you're doing?'

'I'm digging up potatoes, sor.'

'Potatoes? Those tiny things? You call them potatoes? Back home in Milwaukee we have potatoes ten times that size!'

'Yes, sor. But you see, we only grow them to fit our mouths!'

When the time came for his child to be baptised Mike Mulligan proudly stood by the font in St Mary's church.

'Now then,' said Father O'Malley, 'what are we going to call the little one?'

'Hazel,' said Mulligan, with a smile.

'Lord have mercy,' said the priest. 'All the saints in heaven, and you're naming her after a nut!'

*I'm an atheist
and I thank God for it.*

George Bernard Shaw

'I've just bought a new clock,' said O'Toole to the barkeeper. 'It goes eight days without winding.'

'How long does it go if you do wind it?' asked the barman.

Maloney was seen trying to shin up a massive flagpole, with little success.

'What's the problem?' asked O'Donnell.

'The boss wants me to measure this pole,' said Maloney.

'Well, save yourself the effort and lay the pole down, why don't you?' O'Donnell replied.

'No good,' said Maloney. 'He wanted the height not the length.'

'At the time of the accident you were in charge of the bus?' asked the judge.

'Yes, I was, Your Honour,' replied Kelly.

'Can you tell the court what happened?'

'I can't, sor,' said Kelly. 'At the time I was upstairs collecting the fares!'

'And what does your husband do?' asked Moira.

'He works in the clock factory,' replied Katherine. 'He sits down and makes faces all day!'

Two Irishmen

saw a sign that said

'Tree fellers wanted'.

The first said to the second,

'If Mick were with

us, we'd have got the job!'

McGee had asked O'Leary for the hand of his eldest daughter.

'Can you support a family?' O'Leary asked him.

'Oh yes, I should think so,' replied McGee.

'Well, there are six of us, you know!' said his future father-in-law.

The Casey brothers stared out across the sea.

'Look at all that water,' said Billy.

'Aye,' said Jimmy. 'And that there's just the top!'

The priest, a Jesuit no less, stood in the pulpit, high above the congregation and bellowed about sin, damnation and kingdom come. For twenty minutes he roared out a tirade, whilst pounding the pulpit with both hands.

Eventually young Brian O'Connor, six years old, turned to his mother and said, 'Mammy, what will we do if he gets out of there?'

Conor O'Reilly lay in hospital, bandaged head to foot, with just two small slits for his eyes.

'What happened to you?' asked his mate, O'Grady.

'I staggered out of the pub and a lorry hit me a glancing blow and knocked me through a window.'

'God in heaven!' said O'Grady. 'Thank the Lord you were wearing those bandages or you'd have been cut to pieces!'

There was once an Irishman who was so excited after he read about waterskiing, he went looking for a lake with a slope on it.

Michael and Sean are sitting in the pub. Sean says, 'My long-lost brother is coming home at last tomorrow. He sent me a letter saying he'll be at Dublin Airport at eight in the evening.'

'If he's been away so long,' says Michael, 'how will you know him?'

'To be sure, I won't!' replied Sean. 'But he'll know me because I've never been away at all!'

Francis Finnegan went into the local DIY shop. 'I want some six by four timber for me new barn,' he said.

'We don't call it that now,' said the manager. 'Since we went metric you need to ask for 15.2 cm by 10.16 cm. And if you want any it's two euros a foot!'

The priest was concerned when the farmer told him that, in support of women's rights, he had employed a farm girl to work with his staff of five farmhands.

'Tell me, Seamus, is she chaste?' asked the clergyman.

Seamus replied, 'Jesus and she is, Father, all over the farmyard!'

'What's wrong with Dylan?' asked Father Donnall.

His wife replied, 'I don't know, Father. Yesterday he swallowed a spoon and he hasn't stirred since!'

> **SHEEPDOG FOR SALE.
> WILL EAT ANYTHING. VERY
> FOND OF CHILDREN.**

Notice in a local newspaper

Murray rang Aer Lingus and asked how long it took to fly from Dublin to London.

'Just a minute, sir,' said the girl on the desk.

'Thank you,' said Murray, and hung up.

''Scuse me, landlord, but do lemons have legs?' asked Paddy.

'I don't think they do, why do you ask?'

'Well, then I think I've squeezed your budgie into me gin!'

It was the young Irishman's first date and his girl was a little more experienced than him, to say the least. They lay at the bottom of the hill and caressed. Impatiently, she took his hand, put it on her knee and said, 'What about going a bit higher?' The young farmer stood up and started climbing the hill.

'Oh Father,' said Mary O'Cleary to the new priest. 'Your sermons are indeed a wonder to behold. Sure we didn't know what sin was till you came to the parish!'

It is the skill of

an Irishman

to be able to argue either

side of a question

– often at the same time!

A knock came at the farmhouse door and the farmer's son answered it. The man at the door said, 'I've come to ask about the donkey for sale.'

The boy shouted into the kitchen, 'Da, you're wanted!'

The city visitor to Donal's farm was very well versed in farm animals, or so he thought.

He paused in front of one animal and asked the farmer, 'Why has that cow got no horns?'

The farmer told him, 'Some cows have their horns cut off when they're calves. Some don't grow horns at all. But the one you're looking at has none because it is a sheep.'

As Mrs O'Connell entered her home, she looked up to see a ceiling 16 feet high.

'God in heaven!' she said to her husband, Pat. 'When you said you were going to knock two rooms into one I didn't think you meant vertically!'

Downing his drink, Steve Quinn turned to the barman and said, 'I must be off. I'm taking night school classes in Chinese.'

'Why's that?' asked the barman.

'Well, we've just adopted a Chinese baby and I want to know what she says when she grows up,' replied Quinn.

Have you heard

about the Irish boomerang?

It doesn't come back

– it just sings songs about how

much it wants to.

Seamus Maloney didn't realise it, but when drunk, he talked in his sleep. He found out about his affliction when one fateful night he returned home the worse for wear and fell asleep as soon as he hit the pillow. All night through, midst his snores, he kept his wife awake muttering, 'Ramona, oh Ramona! Ramonaaaa!'

In the morning his wife woke him and said, 'It's time for work. And who's that Ramona you were talking about in your sleep?'

'Ramona?' said Maloney, a little taken aback. 'Ramona? That's not a woman.

That's a horse. A feller in the pub gave me a tip in the 3.30 at Haydock Races, a horse called Ramona.'

Seamus went to work feeling smug about the way he'd pulled the wool over his missus' eyes. Coming home that evening, he was greeted by his bags, all packed, standing outside the front door.

'Jesus,' he said to his wife, 'what's happened?'

She replied through gritted teeth, 'The horse called!'

Shane ran along the corridor of the train, opening every compartment door and asking, 'Is there a priest or a vicar here?'

After four attempts he came to a compartment where a man said, 'I'm a rabbi if that's any good?'

'No, thank you,' said Shane. 'I'm looking for a corkscrew!'

Fifty per cent o' me

farmhouse guests

came from abroad.

The other fella

came from Dublin.

An Englishman, an Irishman and a Scotsman each put an odd number of spoons of sugar in his tea. Altogether, they put 16 spoons of sugar in their tea. How come?

The Englishman put in one spoon, the Scotsman put in one spoon and the Irishman put in 14 spoons which is a very odd number of spoons of sugar to put in tea!

'The boss just called,' said O'Reilly. 'He says they're sending us a thousand bricks later today.'

'Jesus!' said Finnegan. 'How many bricks is in a thousand?'

'I don't know,' said O'Reilly, 'but there must be millions!'

Brendan is a

hardened drinker,

but every few years, he'll

take an alcoholiday!

There once was a mean farmer who got married, brought his young bride to the station and handed her a ticket to Dublin. 'Off you go on your honeymoon, girl,' he said. 'It would be a waste o' money if I went, for I was there before.'

'How far is it to the next village?' the American tourist asked Jimmy.

'It's about seven miles,' said Jimmy. 'But it's only five if you run!'

Father O'Brien
stubbed his toe
and stumbled in
the middle of a baptism.
From then on the
girl was known as Mary
Oops O'Grady.

'We're a man short,' the foreman said to Patrick O'Doon.

'Why don't you employ me brother,' suggested O'Doon. 'He can do the work of two men!'

'Alright,' said the boss. 'Send him in tomorrow and then you're sacked!'

'Anyone who can guess how many ducks are in this bag can have the both of them,' said Reagan.

'Three,' said O'Cleary.

'That's near enough,' said Reagan.

Two eighty-year-olds were sat together watching TV.

'Brian, me darlin',' said Faye. 'Would you do me a favour? Would you go and get me some ice cream?'

'Sure' said Brian.

'Shall I write it down for you?' asked Faye. 'Your memory's not what it was.'

'Don't be stupid, woman. I can remember a simple thing like a bowl of ice cream,' laughed Brian.

'True, but I was thinking of having a little raspberry sauce on it, so I'd better write it down.'

'Jesus,' said Brian. 'I'm no fool you know. I can remember ice cream with raspberry sauce.'

'Aye, but do you know those hundreds and thousands? I was thinking of a sprinkling of them on top. I'd best draw a picture,' said Faye.

'You will not!' shouted Brian. 'I can remember ice cream, raspberry sauce and hundreds and thousands. Just hang on a minute.'

Faye waited. Forty minutes later, Brian came in carrying a plate. On the plate was an egg, bacon and sausages.

'See, I should have written everything down!' said Faye.

'Why's that?' asked Brian.

'You've forgotten me toast!'

The fickleness of the women I love is only equalled by the infernal constancy of the women who love me.

George Bernard Shaw

Paddy caught a young boy in the act of robbing his orchard. He grabbed the boy by the shoulder and said, 'If you were my boy, I'd send you to a reformatory.'

The boy replied, 'If that were true, I'd volunteer to go!'

The Irishman was very proud of his eldest daughter.

'Whichever man marries me daughter will get a prize,' he said.

'What will it be?' came the question from the back of the room.

SEAMUS:
me boy just got the
clock going after
nearly thirty years.

MICK:
he must have been very
young when he started!

An Englishman, a Scotsman, and an Irishman walk into a pub together. Each buys a pint of Guinness. Just as they are about to enjoy their creamy beverage, a fly lands in each of their pints, and gets stuck in the thick head.

The Englishman pushes his beer away in disgust, saying, 'I can't drink that!'

The Scotsman fishes the fly out of his beer, and continues drinking it, as if nothing has happened.

The Irishman, too, picks the fly out of his drink, holds it out over the beer, and yells, 'SPIT IT OUT!'

Irish Alzheimer's:

You forget everything

but the grudges!

What's the difference between

a Cork farmer

and a coconut?

You can get a drink

out of a coconut.

A man from Dublin went to visit London for the first time. Finding himself in the underground late one night, he saw a notice: 'Dogs must be carried on the escalator.' 'Great,' he thought to himself, 'where am I going to find a dog at this time o' night?'

If you're interested in finding out more about our humour books, follow us on Twitter: @SummersdaleLOL

www.summersdale.com